CW01083223

The Sonnets Of John Keats

John Keats

Nabu Public Domain Reprints:

You are holding a reproduction of an original work published before 1923 that is in the public domain in the United States of America, and possibly other countries. You may freely copy and distribute this work as no entity (individual or corporate) has a copyright on the body of the work. This book may contain prior copyright references, and library stamps (as most of these works were scanned from library copies). These have been scanned and retained as part of the historical artifact.

This book may have occasional imperfections such as missing or blurred pages, poor pictures, errant marks, etc. that were either part of the original artifact, or were introduced by the scanning process. We believe this work is culturally important, and despite the imperfections, have elected to bring it back into print as part of our continuing commitment to the preservation of printed works worldwide. We appreciate your understanding of the imperfections in the preservation process, and hope you enjoy this valuable book.

THE SONNETS OF JOHN KEATS 🦋 🦋

PUBLISHED BY GEORGE BELL
& SONS, LONDON. MDCCCXCVIII

INDEX OF FIRST LINES.

3809
.386

822719

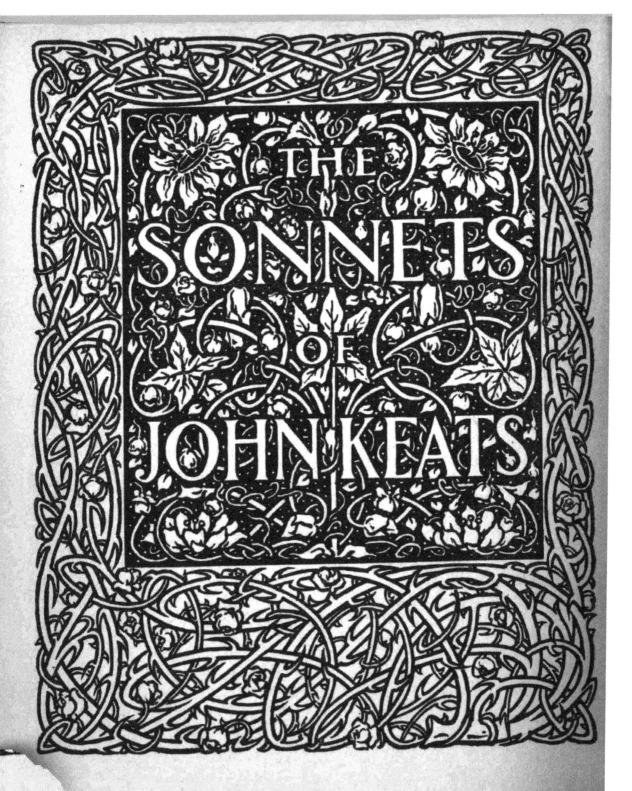

THE SONNETS OF JOHN KEATS

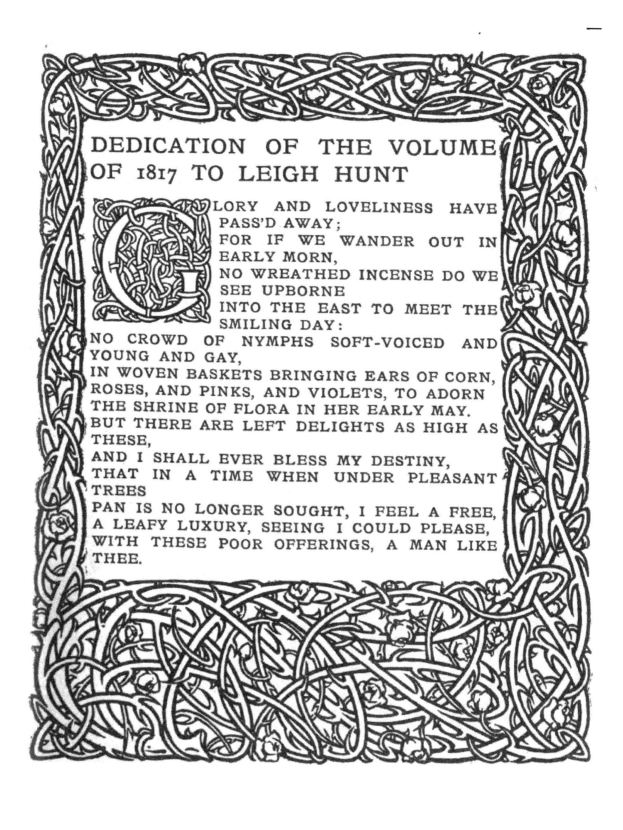

DEDICATION OF THE VOLUME
OF 1817 TO LEIGH HUNT

GLORY AND LOVELINESS HAVE
PASS'D AWAY;
FOR IF WE WANDER OUT IN
EARLY MORN,
NO WREATHED INCENSE DO WE
SEE UPBORNE
INTO THE EAST TO MEET THE
SMILING DAY:
NO CROWD OF NYMPHS SOFT-VOICED AND
YOUNG AND GAY,
IN WOVEN BASKETS BRINGING EARS OF CORN,
ROSES, AND PINKS, AND VIOLETS, TO ADORN
THE SHRINE OF FLORA IN HER EARLY MAY.
BUT THERE ARE LEFT DELIGHTS AS HIGH AS
THESE,
AND I SHALL EVER BLESS MY DESTINY,
THAT IN A TIME WHEN UNDER PLEASANT
TREES
PAN IS NO LONGER SOUGHT, I FEEL A FREE,
A LEAFY LUXURY, SEEING I COULD PLEASE,
WITH THESE POOR OFFERINGS, A MAN LIKE
THEE.

CHATTERTON! how very sad
thy fate!
Dear child of sorrow — son of
misery!
How soon the film of death ob-
scured that eye,
Whence Genius mildly flash'd, and high debate.
How soon that voice, majestic and elate,
Melted in dying numbers! Oh! how nigh
Was night to thy fair morning. Thou didst die
A half-blown flow'ret which cold blasts amate.
But this is past: thou art among the stars
Of highest heaven: to thy rolling spheres
Thou sweetest singest: nought thy hymning mars,
Above the ingrate world and human fears.
On earth the good man base detraction bars
From thy fair name, and waters it with tears.

YRON! how sweetly sad thy melody!
Attuning still the soul to tenderness,
As if soft Pity, with unusual stress,
Had touch'd her plaintive lute, and thou being by,
Hadst caught the tones, nor suffer'd them to die.
O'ershadowing sorrow doth not make thee less
Delightful: thou thy griefs dost dress
With a bright halo, shining beamily,
As when a cloud the golden moon doth veil,
Its sides are tinged with a resplendent glow,
Through the dark robe oft amber rays prevail,
And like fair veins in sable marble flow.
Still warble, dying swan! still tell the tale,
The enchanting tale, the tale of pleasing woe.

3   B

SPENSER! a jealous honourer of thine,
A forester deep in thy midmost trees,
Did, last eve, ask my promise to refine
Some English, that might strive thine ear to please.
But, Elfin-poet! 'tis impossible
For an inhabitant of wintry earth
To rise, like Phœbus, with a golden quill,
Fire-wing'd, and make a morning in his mirth.
It is impossible to 'scape from toil
O' the sudden, and receive thy spiriting:
The flower must drink the nature of the soil
Before it can put forth its blossoming:
Be with me in the summer days, and I
Will for thine honour and his pleasure try.

4

TO MY BROTHER GEORGE

MANY the wonders I this day have
    seen:
The sun, when first he kist away
    the tears
That fill'd the eyes of Morn;—the
    laurell'd peers
Who from the feathery gold of evening lean;—
The Ocean with its vastness, its blue green,
Its ships, its rocks, its caves, its hopes, its fears,
Its voice mysterious, which whoso hears
Must think on what will be, and what has been.
E'en now, dear George, while this for you I write,
Cynthia is from her silken curtains peeping
So scantly, that it seems her bridal night,
And she her half-discover'd revels keeping.
But what, without the social thought of thee,
Would be the wonders of the sky and sea?

S from the darkening gloom a silver
dove
Upsoars, and darts into the eastern
light,
On pinions that nought moves but
pure delight,
So fled thy soul into the realms above,
Regions of peace and everlasting love ;
Where happy spirits, crown'd with circlets bright
Of starry beam, and gloriously bedight,
Taste the high joy none but the blest can prove.
There thou or joinest the immortal quire
In melodies that even heaven fair
Fill with superior bliss, or, at desire,
Of the omnipotent Father, cleavest the air
On holy message sent—What pleasure's higher ?
Wherefore does any grief our joy impair ?
1816.

6

WRITTEN ON A SUMMER EVENING

THE church bells toll a melancholy round,
   Calling the people to some other prayers,
   Some other gloominess, more dreadful cares,
More hearkening to the sermon's horrid sound.
Surely the mind of man is closely bound
In some blind spell: seeing that each one tears
Himself from fireside joys and Lydian airs,
And converse high of those with glory crown'd.
Still, still they toll, and I should feel a damp,
A chill as from a tomb, did I not know
That they are dying like an outburnt lamp,—
That 'tis their sighing, wailing, ere they go
Into oblivion—that fresh flowers will grow,
And many glories of immortal stamp.
1816.

7

TO G. A. W.

NYMPH of the downward smile and
sidelong glance!
In what diviner moments of the
day
Art thou most lovely?—when gone
far astray
Into the labyrinths of sweet utterance,
Or when serenely wandering in a trance
Of sober thought? Or when starting away,
With careless robe to meet the morning ray,
Thou sparest the flowers in thy mazy dance?
Haply 'tis when thy ruby lips part sweetly,
And so remain, because thou listenest:
But thou to please wert nurtured so completely
That I can never tell what mood is best,
I shall as soon pronounce which Grace more neatly
Trips it before Apollo than the rest.

8

TO ——

AD I a man's fair form, then might my sighs
    Be echoed swiftly through that ivory shell,
    Thine ear, and find thy gentle heart; so well
Would passion arm me for the enterprise:
But ah! I am no knight whose foeman dies;
No cuirass glistens on my bosom's swell;
I am no happy shepherd of the dell
Whose lips have trembled with a maiden's eyes.
Yet must I doat upon thee,—call thee sweet,
Sweeter by far than Hybla's honied roses
When steep'd in dew rich to intoxication.
Ah! I will taste that dew, for me 'tis meet,
And when the moon her pallid face discloses,
I'll gather some by spells, and incantation.

9

TO A FRIEND WHO SENT ME SOME ROSES

S late I rambled in the happy fields,
What time the skylark shakes the
tremulous dew
From his lush clover covert;—
when anew
Adventurous knights take up their
dinted shields;
I saw the sweetest flower wild nature yields,
A fresh-blown musk-rose; 'twas the first that
threw
Its sweets upon the summer: graceful it grew
As is the wand that queen Titania wields.
And, as I feasted on its fragrancy,
I thought the garden-rose it far excell'd;
But when, O Wells! thy roses came to me,
My sense with their deliciousness was spell'd:
Soft voices had they, that with tender plea
Whisper'd of peace, and truth, and friendliness
unquell'd.

10

SOLITUDE! if I must with thee dwell,

Let it not be among the jumbled heap

Of murky buildings: climb with me the steep,—

Nature's observatory—whence the dell,

In flowery slopes, its river's crystal swell,

May seem a span; let me thy vigils keep

'Mongst boughs pavilion'd, where the deer's swift leap

Startles the wild bee from the foxglove bell.

But though I'll gladly trace these scenes with thee,

Yet the sweet converse of an innocent mind,

Whose words are images of thoughts refined,

Is my soul's pleasure; and it sure must be

Almost the highest bliss of human-kind,

When to thy haunts two kindred spirits flee.

11

OH! how I love, on a fair summer's eve,
When streams of light pour down the golden west,
And on the balmy zephyrs tranquil rest
The silver clouds, far—far away to leave
All meaner thoughts, and take a sweet reprieve
From little cares; to find, with easy quest,
A fragrant wild, with Nature's beauty drest,
And there into delight my soul deceive.
There warm my breast with patriotic lore,
Musing on Milton's fate—on Sydney's bier—
Till their stern forms before my mind arise:
Perhaps on wing of Poesy upsoar,
Full often dropping a delicious tear,
When some melodious sorrow spells mine eyes.
1816.

12

TO A YOUNG LADY WHO SENT ME
A LAUREL CROWN

FRESH morning gusts have blown away all fear
From my glad bosom,—now from gloominess
I mount for ever—not an atom less
Than the proud laurel shall content my bier.
No! by the eternal stars! or why sit here
In the Sun's eye, and 'gainst my temples press
Apollo's very leaves, woven to bless
By thy white fingers and thy spirit clear.
Lo! who dares say, "Do this"? Who dares call down
My will from its high purpose? Who say, "Stand,"
Or "Go"? This mighty moment I would frown
On abject Cæsars—not the stoutest band
Of mailed heroes should tear off my crown:
Yet would I kneel and kiss thy gentle hand.

13

WRITTEN ON THE DAY THAT MR. LEIGH HUNT LEFT PRISON

WHAT though, for showing truth to flatter'd state,
Kind Hunt was shut in prison, yet has he,
In his immortal spirit, been as free
As the sky-searching lark, and as elate.
Minion of grandeur! think you he did wait?
Think you he nought but prison-walls did see,
Till, so unwilling, thou unturn'dst the key?
Ah, no! far happier, nobler was his fate!
In Spenser's halls he stray'd, and bowers fair,
Culling enchanted flowers; and he flew
With daring Milton through the fields of air:
To regions of his own his genius true
Took happy flights. Who shall his fame impair
When thou art dead, and all thy wretched crew?

TO KOSCIUSKO

GOOD Kosciusko! thy great name alone
Is a full harvest whence to reap high feeling;
It comes upon us like the glorious pealing
Of the wide spheres—an everlasting tone.
And now it tells me, that in worlds unknown,
The names of heroes, burst from clouds concealing,
Are changed to harmonies, for ever stealing
Through cloudless blue, and round each silver throne.
It tells me too, that on a happy day,
When some good spirit walks upon the earth,
Thy name with Alfred's, and the great of yore,
Gently commingling, gives tremendous birth
To a loud hymn, that sounds far, far away
To where the great God lives for evermore.

15

OW many bards gild the lapses of time!
A few of them have ever been the food
Of my delighted fancy,—I could brood
Over their beauties, earthly, or sublime:
And often, when I sit me down to rhyme,
These will in throngs before my mind intrude:
But no confusion, no disturbance rude
Do they occasion; 'tis a pleasing chime.
So the unnumber'd sounds that evening store;
The songs of birds—the whispering of the leaves—
The voice of waters—the great bell that heaves
With solemn sound,—and thousand others more,
That distance of recognizance bereaves,
Makes pleasing music, and not wild uproar.

ON FIRST LOOKING INTO CHAPMAN'S HOMER

UCH have I travell'd in the realms
of gold,
And many goodly states and king-
doms seen;
Round many western islands have
I been
Which bards in fealty to Apollo hold.
Oft of one wide expanse had I been told,
That deep-brow'd Homer ruled as his demesne:
Yet did I never breathe its pure serene
Till I heard Chapman speak out loud and bold:
Then felt I like some watcher of the skies
When a new planet swims into his ken;
Or like stout Cortez when with eagle eyes
He stared at the Pacific—and all his men
Look'd at each other with a wild surmise—
Silent, upon a peak in Darien.

EEN fitful gusts are whispering here and there
Among the bushes, half leafless and dry;
The stars look very cold about the sky,
And I have many miles on foot to fare;
Yet feel I little of the cool bleak air,
Or of the dead leaves rustling drearily,
Or of those silver lamps that burn on high,
Or of the distance from home's pleasant lair:
For I am brimfull of the friendliness
That in a little cottage I have found;
Of fair-hair'd Milton's eloquent distress,
And all his love for gentle Lycid drown'd;
Of lovely Laura in her light green dress,
And faithful Petrarch gloriously crown'd.

ON LEAVING SOME FRIENDS AT AN EARLY HOUR

IVE me a golden pen, and let me lean
On heap'd-up flowers, in regions clear, and far;
Bring me a tablet whiter than a star,
Or hand of hymning angel, when 'tis seen
The silver strings of heavenly harp atween:
And let there glide by many a pearly car,
Pink robes, and wavy hair, and diamond jar,
And half-discover'd wings, and glances keen.
The while let music wander round my ears,
And as it reaches each delicious ending,
Let me write down a line of glorious tone,
And full of many wonders of the spheres:
For what a height my spirit is contending!
'Tis not content so soon to be alone.

APPY is England! I could be content
To see no other verdure than its own;
To feel no other breezes than are blown
Through its tall woods with high romances blent;
Yet do I sometimes feel a languishment
For skies Italian, and an inward groan
To sit upon an Alp as on a throne,
And half forget what world or worldling meant.
Happy is England, sweet her artless daughters;
Enough their simple loveliness for me,
Enough their whitest arms in silence clinging.
Yet do I often warmly burn to see
Beauties of deeper glance, and hear their singing,
And float with them about the summer waters.

TO MY BROTHERS

SMALL, busy flames play through
the fresh-laid coals,
And their faint cracklings o'er our
silence creep
Like whispers of the household
gods that keep
A gentle empire o'er fraternal souls.
And while, for rhymes, I search around the poles,
Your eyes are fix'd, as in poetic sleep,
Upon the lore so voluble and deep,
That aye at fall of night our care condoles.
This is your birth-day, Tom, and I rejoice
That thus it passes smoothly, quietly:
Many such eves of gently whispering noise
May we together pass, and calmly try
What are this world's true joys,—ere the great
Voice
From its fair face shall bid our spirits fly.
November 18, 1816.

ON THE GRASSHOPPER AND CRICKET

THE poetry of earth is never dead :
When all the birds are faint with
the hot sun,
And hide in cooling trees, a voice
will run
From hedge to hedge about the
new-mown mead.
That is the grasshopper's—he takes the lead
In summer luxury,—he has never done
With his delights, for when tired out with fun,
He rests at ease beneath some pleasant weed.
The poetry of earth is ceasing never :
On a lone winter evening, when the frost
Has wrought a silence, from the stove there shrills
The Cricket's song, in warmth increasing ever,
And seems to one in drowsiness half-lost,
The Grasshopper's among some grassy hills.
December 30, 1816.

ADDRESSED TO HAYDON

HIGH-MINDEDNESS, a jealousy
for good,
A loving-kindness for the great
man's fame,
Dwells here and there with people
of no name,
In noisome alley, and in pathless wood:
And where we think the truth least understood,
Oft may be found a " singleness of aim,"
That ought to frighten into hooded shame
A money-mongering, pitiable brood.
How glorious this affection for the cause
Of steadfast genius, toiling gallantly!
What when a stout unbending champion awes
Envy and malice to their native sty?
Unnumber'd souls breathe out a still applause,
Proud to behold him in his country's eye.

23

ADDRESSED TO THE SAME

GREAT spirits now on earth are so-
journing:
He of the cloud, the cataract, the
lake,
Who on Helvellyn's summit, wide
awake,
Catches his freshness from Archangel's wing;:
He of the rose, the violet, the spring,
The social smile, the chain for Freedom's sake:
And lo! whose steadfastness would never take
A meaner sound than Raphael's whispering.
And other spirits there are standing apart
Upon the forehead of the age to come ;
These, these will give the world another heart,
And other pulses. Hear ye not the hum
Of mighty workings ?——
Listen awhile, ye nations, and be dumb.

FTER dark vapours have oppress'd our plains
For a long dreary season, comes a day
Born of the gentle South, and clears away
From the sick heavens all unseemly stains.
The anxious month, relieved from its pains,
Takes as a long-lost right the feel of May,
The eye-lids with the passing coolness play,
Like rose-leaves with the drip of summer rains.
And calmest thoughts come round us—as of leaves
Budding—fruit ripening in stillness—autumn suns
Smiling at eve upon the quiet sheaves,—
Sweet Sappho's cheek, — a sleeping infant's breath,—
The gradual sand that through an hour-glass runs,—
A woodland rivulet,—a Poet's death.

Jan. 1817.   25

ON SEEING THE ELGIN MARBLES FOR THE FIRST TIME

MY spirit is too weak; mortality
Weighs heavily on me like unwilling sleep,
And each imagined pinnacle and steep
Of godlike hardship tells me I must die
Like a sick eagle looking at the sky.
Yet 'tis a gentle luxury to weep,
That I have not the cloudy winds to keep
Fresh for the opening of the morning's eye.
Such dim-conceived glories of the brain
Bring round the heart an indescribable feud;
So do these wonders a most dizzy pain,
That mingles Grecian grandeur with the rude
Wasting of old Time—with a billowy main,
A sun, a shadow of a magnitude.

1817.

TO HAYDON

(WITH THE FOREGOING)

AYDON ! forgive me that I cannot speak
Definitively of these mighty things ;
Forgive me, that I have not eagle's wings,
That what I want I know not where to seek.
And think that I would not be over-meek,
In rolling out upfollow'd thunderings,
Even to the steep of Heliconian springs,
Were I of ample strength for such a freak.
Think, too, that all these numbers should be thine;
Whose else ? In this who touch thy vesture's hem ?
For, when men stared at what was most divine
With brainless idiotism and o'erwise phlegm,
Thou hadst beheld the full Hesperian shine
Of their star in the east, and gone to worship them !

HEN I have fears that I may cease
to be
Before my pen has glean'd my
teeming brain,
Before high-piled books, in char-
act'ry,
Hold like full garners the full-ripen'd grain;
When I behold, upon the night's starr'd face,
Huge cloudy symbols of a high romance,
And feel that I may never live to trace
Their shadows, with the magic hand of chance;
And when I feel, fair creature of an hour!
That I shall never look upon thee more,
Never have relish in the faery power
Of unreflecting love!—then on the shore
Of the wide world I stand alone, and think,
Till Love and Fame to nothingness do sink.
1817.

ON LEIGH HUNT'S POEM, THE
"STORY OF RIMINI"

WHO loves to peer up at the morn-
ing sun,
With half-shut eyes and comfort-
able cheek,
Let him, with this sweet tale, full
often seek
For meadows where the little rivers run;
Who loves to linger with that brightest one
Of Heaven—Hesperus—let him lowly speak
These numbers to the night, and starlight meek,
Or moon, if that her hunting be begun.
He who knows these delights, and too is prone
To moralize upon a smile or tear,
Will find at once a region of his own,
A bower for his spirit, and will steer
To alleys, where the fir-tree drops its cone,
Where robins hop, and fallen leaves are sear.
1817.

WRITTEN ON A BLANK SPACE AT THE END OF CHAUCER'S TALE OF "THE FLOWRE AND THE LEFE"

THIS pleasant tale is like a little
    copse :
The honied lines so freshly inter-
    lace,
To keep the reader in so sweet a
    place,
So that he here and there full-hearted stops ;
And oftentimes he feels the dewy drops
Come cool and suddenly against his face,
And, by the wandering melody, may trace
Which way the tender-legged linnet hops.
Oh ! what a power has white Simplicity !
What mighty power has this gentle story !
I, that do ever feel athirst for glory,
Could at this moment be content to lie
Meekly upon the grass, as those whose sobbings
Were heard of none beside the mournful robins.
1817.

ON A PICTURE OF LEANDER

COME hither, all sweet maidens soberly,
Down-looking aye, and with a chasten'd light
Hid in the fringes of your eyelids white,
And meekly let your fair hands joined be,
As if so gentle that ye could not see,
Untouch'd, a victim of your beauty bright,
Sinking away to his young spirit's night,
Sinking bewilder'd 'mid the dreary sea:
'Tis young Leander toiling to his death;
Nigh swooning, he doth purse his weary lips
For Hero's cheek, and smiles against her smile.
O horrid dream! see how his body dips,
Dead-heavy; arms and shoulders gleam awhile:
He's gone; up bubbles all his amorous breath!

31

ON THE SEA

IT keeps eternal whisperings around
Desolate shores, and with its mighty swell
Gluts twice ten thousand caverns, till the spell
Of Hecate leaves them their old shadowy sound.
Often 'tis in such gentle temper found,
That scarcely will the very smallest shell
Be moved for days from whence it sometime fell,
When last the winds of heaven were unbound.
Oh ye! who have your eye-balls vex'd and tired,
Feast them upon the wideness of the Sea;
Oh ye! whose ears are dinn'd with uproar rude,
Or fed too much with cloying melody,—
Sit ye near some old cavern's mouth, and brood
Until ye start, as if the sea-nymphs quired!
Aug. 1817.

TO THE NILE

ON of the old Moon-mountains
African!
Chief of the Pyramid and Croco-
dile!
We call thee fruitful, and that very
while
A desert fills our seeing's inward span:
Nurse of swart nations since the world began,
Art thou so fruitful? or dost thou beguile
Such men to honour thee, who, worn with toil,
Rest for a space 'twixt Cairo and Decan?
O may dark fancies err! They surely do;
'Tis ignorance that makes a barren waste
Of all beyond itself. Thou dost bedew
Green rushes like our rivers, and dost taste
The pleasant sunrise. Green isles hast thou too,
And to the sea as happily dost haste.
1818.

ON VISITING THE TOMB OF BURNS

THE town, the churchyard, and the setting sun,
The clouds, the trees, the rounded hills all seem,
Though beautiful, cold—strange—as in a dream,
I dreamed long ago, now new begun.
The short-lived paly Summer is but won
From Winter's ague, for one hour's gleam;
Though sapphire-warm, their stars do never beam:
All is cold Beauty; pain is never done:
For who has mind to relish, Minos-wise,
The Real of Beauty, free from that dead hue
Sickly imagination and sick pride
Cast wan upon it! Burns! with honour due
I oft have honour'd thee. Great shadow! hide
Thy face; I sin against thy native skies.
1818.

WRITTEN IN BURNS' COTTAGE

THIS mortal body of a thousand days
Now fills, O Burns, a space in thine
own room,
Where thou didst dream alone on
budded bays,
Happy and thoughtless of thy day
of doom !
My pulse is warm with thine own Barley-bree,
My head is light with pledging a great soul,
My eyes are wandering, and I cannot see,
Fancy is dead and drunken at its goal ;
Yet can I stamp my foot upon thy floor,
Yet can I ope thy window-sash to find
The meadow thou hast tramped o'er and o'er,—
Yet can I think of thee till thought is blind,—
Yet can I gulp a bumper to thy name,—
O smile among the shades, for this is fame !
1818.

TO AILSA ROCK

HEARKEN, thou craggy ocean-
pyramid,
Give answer by thy voice—the
sea-fowls' screams!
When were thy shoulders mantled
in huge streams?
When from the sun was thy broad forehead hid?
How long is 't since the mighty Power bid
Thee heave to airy sleep from fathom dreams—
Sleep in the lap of thunder or sunbeams—
Or when grey clouds are thy cold coverlid!
Thou answer'st not; for thou art dead asleep.
Thy life is but two dead eternities,
The last in air, the former in the deep!
First with the whales, last with the eagle-skies!
Drown'd wast thou till an earthquake made thee
steep,
Another cannot wake thy giant-size!

1818. 36

BEN NEVIS

EAD me a lesson, Muse, and speak it loud
Upon the top of Nevis, blind in mist!
I look into the chasms, and a shroud
Vapourous doth hide them,—just so much I wist
Mankind do know of hell; I look o'erhead,
And there is sullen mist,—even so much
Mankind can tell of heaven; mist is spread
Before the earth, beneath me,—even such,
Even so vague is man's sight of himself!
Here are the craggy stones beneath my feet,—
Thus much I know that, a poor witless elf,
I tread on them,—that all my eye doth meet
Is mist and crag, not only on this height,
But in the world of thought and mental might!
1818.

TO one who has been long in city pent,
'Tis very sweet to look into the fair
And open face of heaven,—to breathe a prayer
Full in the smile of the blue firmament.
Who is more happy, when, with heart's content,
Fatigued he sinks into some pleasant lair
Of wavy grass, and reads a debonair
And gentle tale of love and languishment?
Returning home at evening, with an ear
Catching the notes of Philomel,—an eye
Watching the sailing cloudlet's bright career,
He mourns that day so soon has glided by,
E'en like the passage of an angel's tear
That falls through the clear ether silently.

THE HUMAN SEASONS

FOUR Seasons fill the measure of
the year;
There are four seasons in the mind
of man:
He has his lusty Spring, when
fancy clear
Takes in all beauty with an easy span:
He has his Summer, when luxuriously
Spring's honied cud of youthful thought he loves
To ruminate, and by such dreaming high
Is nearest unto Heaven: quiet coves
His soul has in its Autumn, when his wings
He furleth close; contented so to look
On mists in idleness—to let fair things
Pass by unheeded as a threshold brook.
He has his Winter too of pale misfeature,
Or else he would forego his mortal nature.

WRITTEN BEFORE RE-READING KING LEAR

**O** GOLDEN-TONGUED Romance with serene lute!
Fair plumed Syren! Queen of far away!
Leave melodizing on this wintry day,
Shut up thine olden pages, and be mute.
Adieu! for once again the fierce dispute,
Betwixt damnation and impassion'd clay
Must I burn through; once more humbly assay
The bitter-sweet of this Shakespearian fruit.
Chief Poet! and ye clouds of Albion,
Begetters of our deep eternal theme,
When through the old oak Forest I am gone,
Let me not wander in a barren dream,
But when I am consumed in the Fire,
Give me new Phœnix wings to fly at my desire.

Jan., 1818.

FRAGMENT OF A SONNET

ATURE withheld Cassandra in the
skies
For more adornment, a full thou-
sand years;
She took their cream of Beauty,
fairest dies,
And shaped and tinted her above all peers:
Meanwhile Love kept her dearly with his wings,
And underneath their shadow fill'd her eyes
With such a richness that the cloudy Kings
Of high Olympus utter'd slavish sighs.
When from the Heavens I saw her first descend,
My heart took fire, and only burning pains—
They were my pleasures—they my Life's sad end
Love pour'd her beauty into my warm veins.

ANSWER TO A SONNET BY J. H. REYNOLDS, ENDING—

"Dark eyes are dearer far
Than those that mock the hyacinthine bell."

BLUE! 'Tis the life of heaven,—the domain
Of Cynthia,—the wide palace of the sun,—
The tent of Hesperus, and all his train,—
The bosomer of clouds, gold, gray, and dun.
Blue! 'Tis the life of waters:—Ocean
And all its vassal streams, pools numberless,
May rage, and foam, and fret, but never can
Subside, if not to dark-blue nativeness.
Blue! gentle cousin of the forest-green,
Married to green in all the sweetest flowers—
Forget-me-not,—the blue-bell,—and, that queen
Of secrecy, the violet: what strange powers
Hast thou, as a mere shadow! But how great,
When in an Eye thou art alive with fate!

Feb., 1818.

42

TO HOMER

STANDING aloof in giant ignorance,
Of thee I hear and of the Cyclades,
As one who sits ashore and longs perchance
To visit dolphin-coral in deep seas.
So thou wast blind!—but then the veil was rent;
For Jove uncurtain'd Heaven to let thee live,
And Neptune made for thee a spumy tent,
And Pan made sing for thee his forest-hive;
Aye, on the shores of darkness there is light,
And precipices show untrodden green;
There is a budding morrow in midnight;
There is a triple sight in blindness keen;
Such seeing hadst thou, as it once befel,
To Dian, Queen of Earth, and Heaven, and Hell.
1818.

TO JOHN HAMILTON REYNOLDS

 THAT a week could be an age, and we
Felt parting and warm meeting every week,
Then one poor year a thousand years would be,
The flush of welcome ever on the cheek:
So could we live long life in little space,
So time itself would be annihilate,
So a day's journey in oblivious haze
To serve our joys would lengthen and dilate.
O to arrive each Monday morn from Ind!
To land each Tuesday from the rich Levant!
In little time a host of joys to bind,
And keep our souls in one eternal pant!
This morn, my friend, and yester-evening taught
Me how to harbour such a happy thought.

TO A LADY SEEN FOR A FEW MOMENTS
AT VAUXHALL

IME'S sea hath been five years at
its slow ebb;
Long hours have to and fro let
creep the sand,
Since I was tangled in thy beauty's
web,
And snared by the ungloving of thine hand.
And yet I never look on midnight sky,
But I behold thine eyes' well memoried light;
I cannot look upon the rose's dye,
But to thy cheek my soul doth take its flight;
I cannot look on any budding flower,
But my fond ear, in fancy at thy lips,
And hearkening for a love-sound, doth devour
Its sweets in the wrong sense:—Thou dost
eclipse
Every delight with sweet remembering,
And grief unto my darling joys dost bring.

TO SLEEP

SOFT embalmer of the still mid-
night!
Shutting, with careful fingers and
benign,
Our gloom-pleased eyes, embower'd
from the light,
Enshaded in forgetfulness divine;
O soothest Sleep! if so it please thee, close,
In midst of this thine hymn, my willing eyes,
Or wait the amen, ere thy poppy throws
Around my bed its lulling charities;
Then save me, or the passed day will shine
Upon my pillow, breeding many woes;
Save me from curious conscience, that still lords
Its strength, for darkness burrowing like a mole;
Turn the key deftly in the oiled wards,
And seal the hushed casket of my soul.
1819.

ON FAME

FAME, like a wayward girl, will still be coy
To those who woo her with too slavish knees,
But makes surrender to some thoughtless boy,
And dotes the more upon a heart at ease;
She is a Gipsy,—will not speak to those
Who have not learnt to be content without her;
A Jilt, whose ear was never whisper'd close,
Who thinks they scandal her who talk about her;
A very Gipsy is she, Nilus-born,
Sister-in-law to jealous Potiphar;
Ye love-sick Bards! repay her scorn for scorn;
Ye Artists lovelorn! madmen that ye are!
Make your best bow to her and bid adieu,
Then, if she likes it, she will follow you.

1819.

ON FAME

"You cannot eat your cake and have it too."—Proverb.

OW fever'd is the man, who cannot look
Upon his mortal days with tem-
perate blood,
Who vexes all the leaves of his
life's book,
And robs his fair name of its maidenhood ;
It is as if the rose should pluck herself,
Or the ripe plum finger its misty bloom,
As if a Naiad, like a meddling elf,
Should darken her pure grot with muddy gloom ;
But the rose leaves herself upon the briar,
For winds to kiss and grateful bees to feed,
And the ripe plum still wears its dim attire ;
The undisturbed lake has crystal space ;
Why then should man, teasing the world for grace,
Spoil his salvation for a fierce miscreed ?
1819.

HY did I laugh to-night? No voice will tell:
No God, no Demon of severe response,
Deigns to reply from Heaven or from Hell.
Then to my human heart I turn at once.
Heart! Thou and I are here, sad and alone;
I say, why did I laugh? O mortal pain!
O Darkness! Darkness! ever must I moan,
To question Heaven and Hell and Heart in vain.
Why did I laugh? I know this Being's lease,
My fancy to its utmost blisses spreads;
Yet would I on this very midnight cease,
And the world's gaudy ensigns see in shreds;
Verse, Fame, and Beauty are intense indeed,
But Death intenser—Death is Life's high meed.
1819.

A DREAM, AFTER READING DANTE'S
EPISODE OF PAOLO AND FRANCESCA

S Hermes once took to his feathers
light,
When lulled Argus, baffled, swoon'd
and slept,
So on a Delphic reed, my idle
spright
So play'd, so charm'd, so conquer'd, so bereft
The dragon-world of all its hundred eyes;
And seeing it asleep, so fled away,
Not to pure Ida with its snow-cold skies,
Nor unto Tempe, where Jove grieved a day;
But to that second circle of sad Hell,
Where in the gust, the whirlwind, and the flaw
Of rain and hail-stones, lovers need not tell
Their sorrows.   Pale were the sweet lips I saw,
Pale were the lips I kiss'd, and fair the form
I floated with, about that melancholy storm.
1819.

F by dull rhymes our English must
be chain'd,
And, like Andromeda, the Sonnet
sweet
Fetter'd, in spite of pained loveli-
ness;
Let us find out, if we must be constrain'd,
Sandals more interwoven and complete
To fit the naked foot of poesy;
Let us inspect the lyre, and weigh the stress
Of every chord, and see what may be gain'd
By ear industrous, and attention meet;
Misers of sound and syllable, no less
Than Midas of his coinage, let us be
Jealous of dead leaves in the bay wreath crown;
So, if we may not let the Muse be free,
She will be bound with garlands of her own.
1819.

HE day is gone, and all its sweets
are gone!
Sweet voice, sweet lips, soft hand,
and softer breast,
Warm breath, light whisper, tender
semi-tone,
Bright eyes, accomplish'd shape, and lang'rous
waist!
Faded the flower and all its budded charms,
Faded the sight of beauty from my eyes,
Faded the shape of beauty from my arms,
Faded the voice, warmth, whiteness, paradise—
Vanish'd unseasonably at shut of eve,
When the dusk holiday—or holinight
Of fragrant-curtain'd love begins to weave
The woof of darkness thick, for hid delight;
But, as I've read love's missal through to-day,
He'll let me sleep, seeing I fast and pray.
1819.

TO FANNY

CRY your mercy—pity—love!— aye, love!
Merciful love that tantalises not,
One-thoughted, never-wandering, guileless love,
Unmask'd, and being seen—without a blot!
O! let me have thee whole,—all—all—be mine!
That shape, that fairness, that sweet minor zest
Of love, your kiss,—those hands, those eyes divine,
That warm, white, lucent, million-pleasured breast,—
Yourself—your soul—in pity give me all,
Withhold no atom's atom or I die,
Or living on, perhaps, your wretched thrall,
Forget, in the mist of idle misery,
Life's purposes,—the palate of my mind
Losing its gust, and my ambition blind!
1819.

HIS LAST SONNET

BRIGHT star! would I were stead-
fast as thou art—
Not in lone splendour hung aloft
the night,
And watching, with eternal lids
apart,
Like Nature's patient, sleepless Eremite,
The moving waters at their priestlike task
Of pure ablution round earth's human shores,
Or gazing on the new soft fallen mask
Of snow upon the mountains and the moors—
No—yet still steadfast, still unchangeable,
Pillow'd upon my fair love's ripening breast,
To feel for ever its soft fall and swell,
Awake for ever in a sweet unrest,
Still, still to hear her tender-taken breath,
And so live ever—or else swoon to death.

1820.

THIS EDITION OF THE SONNETS OF JOHN KEATS,
WITH DECORATED BORDERS AND INITIALS BY
CHRISTOPHER DEAN, IS PUBLISHED BY GEORGE
BELL AND SONS, YORK STREET, COVENT
GARDEN, LONDON, AND PRINTED AT THE
CHISWICK PRESS.   MDCCCXCVIII.

87

Lightning Source UK Ltd.
Milton Keynes UK
UKHW051030091122
411904UK00011B/380